For my Mom, Dad & Harry Holcombe

Love of a Pig

A Comedy

Leslie Caveny

A SAMUEL FRENCH ACTING EDITION

SAMUEL FRENCH

FOUNDED 1830

SAMUELFRENCH.COM
SAMUELFRENCH-LONDON.CO.UK

ISBN 978-0-573-69346-5

www.SamuelFrench.com
www.SamuelFrench-London.co.uk

FOR PRODUCTION ENQUIRIES

UNITED STATES AND CANADA
Info@SamuelFrench.com
1-866-598-8449

UNITED KINGDOM AND EUROPE
Plays@SamuelFrench-London.co.uk
020-7255-4302

Each title is subject to availability from Samuel French, depending upon country of performance. Please be aware that *LOVE OF A PIG* may not be licensed by Samuel French in your territory. Professional and amateur producers should contact the nearest Samuel French office or licensing partner to verify availability.

Love Of A Pig was produced at Theatre West in Hollywood in July 1989 by Doug Carfrae, Catherine MacNeal, and Kevin McMahon; directed by Bob McCracken; production design by Wendy Guidery; lighting design by Lawrence Oberman; musical adaptation by Glenn Mehrbach; production stage manager, Sheila Shaw. The cast (in alphabetical order) was as follows:

Jenny .... Leslie Caveny
Polly & others .... Andrea Iaderosa
Eddie & others .... J. Patrick McCarthy
Joe & others .... Bob McCracken
Mailman & others .... Kevin McMahon
Crystal & others .... Juleen Murray
Amy & others .... Vivien Straus
Mr. Michaels & others .... Paul Anthony Weber

Alternates .... Valri Jackson, Steve Nevil
and Andrew Parks

CHARACTERS

Jenny
Frantic Man
Hank
Alex
Tom
Jessie
Mark
Flower Men (Kevin, Peter, Joshua, Lance)
Mailman
Loverboy
Amy
Crystal
Polly
Sean
David
Henry
Joe
Lady
Man w/Paper
Chrissy
Narrator
Telephone Woman
Military Man
Aerobics Instructor
Pierre
Michelle
Melissa (screaming woman)
Bartender
Lounge Singer
Man In Bar
Eddie
Wolf #1
Wolf #2   (contd.)

Wolf #3
Party Women (three)
Party Men (three)
Jury Foreman
Prosecutor
Defense Attorney
Judge
Bailiff
Hysterical Woman
Boyfriend
Wife
Denial Husband
Gameshow Hostess

Female roles cast as follows:
ONE: **Jenny**
TWO: **Polly**, Chrissy, Michelle, Judge, Party Woman, Telephone Woman
THREE: **Crystal**, Gameshow Hostess, Lady, Party Woman, Prosecutor
FOUR: **Amy**, Jury Foreman, Melissa (screaming woman), Party Woman, Hysterical Woman, Wife

Male roles cast as follows:
ONE: **Eddie**, Loverboy, Jessie, Lance, Man w/Paper, Sean, Military Man, Bartender, Pierre, Wolf #1, Party Man, Denial Husband
TWO: **Joe**, Peter, Tom.
THREE: **Mailman**, Frantic Man, Alex, Joshua, David, Aerobics Instructor, Lounge Singer, Wolf #2, Party Man, Defense Attorney, Boyfriend
FOUR: **Mr. Michaels**, Hank, Mark, Kevin, Man in Bar, Narrator, Wolf #3, Party Man, Bailiff

AUTHOR'S NOTES

In the Los Angeles production, the actors remained on stage throughout the entire play. When an actor was not in a scene he sat in one of the upstage chairs where he was either part of what might be called a "Greek chorus," or just plain watching the play. We kept props, set pieces, costume changes and lighting cues to a minimum. The only light cues involved a spot when Jenny went to the charts. There is a light cue mentioned in the script—a modulating blue spot as Jenny crosses after the Man In Bar scene—but we never did try it. An actor ran all the music cues from a boom box on stage. We had a bright wash of primary colors as a backdrop, and the set pieces, props and costumes were accented with similar colors. The men wore neutral hues, and the women wore brightly colored solids. (Jenny in orange. Crystal in blue. Amy in green. Polly in yellow.) The only additional costume pieces were the Mailman's mailbag and Joe's long brown coat and cap. The instruments were all mimed.

And finally, I'd like to say that keeping the pace up and having fun up on stage counts for a lot with this show. Jenny comes out and says what she means and charts out any inner conflict. She is an optimist on a very focused quest from beginning to end and her highs and lows are driven by true passion. In other words: there are no lulls—everyone just goes for it.

SCENE: *The stage is set with seven colored chairs along the upstage wall, Jenny's bed stage left, and a multi-level bench stage right. The set is representative of Jenny's bedroom, a music room and bar.*

AT RISE: *BEETHOVEN'S FIFTH SYMPHONY is heard. LIGHTS UP on JENNY and seven ACTORS in the chairs. Party laughter.*

JENNY. (*To the audience.*) So everything is great. I have friends who care about me and give me money. I'm an up-and-coming violin soloist. The butcher, the fruit stand man, and the grocery clerk all know me by name—

GROUP. Hi Jenny.

JENNY. —and that's something I've wanted all my life. And people don't gawk at me anymore when I'm walking down the street the way they used to when I was in high school and walked like a starved Neanderthal—Now they all smile and say—

GROUP. Hello.

JENNY. Sometimes my life just chokes me all up. I mean I feel like Mary Tyler Moore. I just wish I had a hat to throw. (*JENNY begins heading toward her apartment.*) And to top it all off, I live in a beautiful, charming, rent-controlled duplex, which is really great, except I live there—here—

9

(As SHE opens the door, GROUP makes desert WIND SOUND. SHE steps in, closes the door—the wind stops.)

JENNY. *—alone.. (JENNY takes a few steps across the room in silence and then stops suddenly as if SHE hears something. Whispers.)* Listen. Do you hear that? *(SHE listens.)* I don't either. I've moved four times in the last two years, in hopes of finding a noisy neighborhood or at least a noisy neighbor. But, it doesn't seem to matter much where I live, or how loud it is outside, the inside of all my apartments always sound the same. I'd like to say I've gotten used to it, but I haven't. The silence just keeps getting louder and louder. I guess the logical answer would be to turn on some music the minute I get home, but— *(SHE mimes turning on stereo, MUSIC BLASTS and SHE shouts over music.)*—I'M SO AFRAID THAT I'LL MISS SOMETHING.

(FRANTIC MAN has entered and is POUNDING on the door. During the following, when the music is UP, HE speaks, when JENNY turns music DOWN, thinking she hears someone, FRANTIC MAN freezes.)

FRANTIC MAN. *(Shouting.)* Jenny, I love you. *(Freeze/silence.)* I need you. I *—(Freeze.)—*want you. Will you mar—*(Freeze.)*—ry—*(Freeze.)* me.

(MUSIC SHUTS OFF and MAN leaves defeated.)

JENNY. I didn't always feel this way. It was a gradual realization that it is entirely possible that I could spend the rest of my life alone. (*JENNY moves to the easel.*) This thought frightened me so I did some thinking and figuring. (*Uncovers pie chart #1.*) I've lived 4,984 days since I hit puberty, and I've spent 4,981 of those nights alone. (*Flips to new pie chart #2, pointing to appropriate sections.*) And if I live to be seventy-five, that's a total 26,700 nights on this earth. I figure I won't marry until I'm thirty-five, giving me 14,240 nights of married life, but for 7,120 of those nights, my husband will be away on business or out having an affair, leaving me alone for the remaining ... I think you get the point. (*SHE crosses to edge of bed and sits.*) But, when fear of spinsterhood overwhelms me, I simply close my eyes and imagine this place as it's meant to be. (*SHE closes her eyes.*)

(*HANK, a violent-tempered young man bursts into Jenny's bedroom area.*)

HANK. Damn it, Jenny, you left the cap off the damn toothpaste. This place is a damn filthy mess!

(*JENNY opens her eyes, HANK vanishes.*)

JENNY. (*Embarrassed.*) No. I mean, I close my eyes and envision this apartment becoming a home. (*Closes eyes.*)
HANK. Damn it, Jenny, get in here and do these damn dishes. This place is a damn filthy mess!
JENNY. (*Frustrated—opens eyes HANK vanishes.*) NO! I MEAN—I close my eyes and envision this place filled with love.

HANK. Damn it, Jenny, how many times do I have to tell you to make the bed. This place is a damn filthy mess!

JENNY. (*Turns on him.*) I don't have time to do everything!!! I have a job, which is more than I can say for you!!!

HANK. How dare you raise your voice to me.

JENNY. I'm sorry, honey, I don't know what got into me.

HANK. I know, I know, it's just that you love me so much, you get all confused.

JENNY. (*In unison with Hank's next line.*) Oh baby, what would I do without you?

HANK. (*Stepping back.*) Oh baby, what would you do without me?

JENNY. (*To the audience.*) Hank—I call him Hank—Hank gives me hope for the future—which is really great, but I have all my hopes in the future. When I tell my friends that I wish I had a boyfriend, they say—

THE WOMEN. Tomorrow tomorrow. Your prince will come.

JENNY. For about two seconds, I find encouragement in that thought. And then I think, well what's going to make tomorrow so different? The 3,000 yesterdays I have just survived, were all tomorrows 3,001 days ago. I mean, my tomorrows are becoming yesterdays at a very rapid rate. Besides, I've had hopes for tomorrows before: When I first came to this grad school, I fell in love with a drummer named Jessie —

(*JESSIE comes center stage.*)

JENNY. —but he was in love with a composer named Tom—

(TOM comes center.)

JENNY. —I had a crush on a guy named Mark—

(MARK comes center. JENNY steps aside and listens:)

JENNY. —but he was sleeping with Jessie. And I went to a movie with a guy named Alex—But —

(ALEX comes center.)

ALEX. Hi, Tom.
TOM. *(Snob.)* Hello, Alex.
ALEX. Hey, Jessie, how ya doin'?
JESSIE. Fine, Alex. How you doin'?
ALEX. Good. Just went to see a movie with Jenny.
TOM. Yeah? What'd you see?
ALEX. We're good friends. We understand each other.
TOM. What movie did you see?
ALEX. You know—I like Jenny a lot. She didn't mind going Dutch. She's so nice. Are you going to her party Friday?
TOM. What movie did you see?
ALEX. You gonna come to her party? I'm sure she wants you all to be there.
MARK. Who the hell is Jenny?!
ALEX. You know Jenny, dontcha? You're all good friends, arentcha?
MARK. Who's Jenny?

JESSIE. Jenny's the jazz violinist who can't get a date.
MARK. Oh yeah—I know her.
ALEX. Oh wow. I thought you and Jenny were good friends.
TOM. What movie did you see?!
JESSIE. When's her party?
ALEX. Who cares. I don't even like her. I was just using her to get closer to you guys.

(THEY laugh and go to their chairs.)

JENNY. It was a no-win situation. But I dealt. And when I first moved into this apartment, I was very optimistic. My first night here, Kevin—this really cute guy from upstairs just drops by—

(KEVIN comes to her door.)

JENNY. —then Peter stops by—

(PETER at her door.)

JENNY. —then Joshua—

(JOSHUA at her door.)

JENNY. —and Lance—

(LANCE at her door.)

JENNY. There they all stood—

(THE FOUR MEN stand single file each with flower in hand.)

FOUR MEN. Hi there—
JENNY. I was ecstatic and overjoyed—songs sung in my head: "Torn Between Four Lovers." My heart did flips and cartwheels and then I heard the dreadful words:
FOUR MEN. Is Mary home?
JENNY. What?
FOUR MEN. Is Mary home?
JENNY. Mary who?
FOUR. Mary Davies.
JENNY. Mary Davies!?
FOUR MEN. Is she home?
JENNY. NO!
FOUR MEN. Oh! *(Their flowers wilt. Disappointed, THEY leave.)*
JENNY. The word must've gotten out that Mary must've moved and they stopped stopping by. And the silence continued to grow. About a month ago, I was ready to give up. I was ready to wallow in my loneliness—model my life after Sylvia Plath's—write a few really depressing poems and swallow a few pills. But, just as I was preparing for my big wallow—

(There is a KNOCK at the door.)

JENNY. There is a knock at the door! Someone is reaching out! Someone has come to save me! I open the door—and it's—*(SHE opens the door with great expectation and then disappointment.)*—the mailman.
MAILMAN. You look disappointed

JENNY. Yeh I am a little disappointed. Nothing personal, you understand?

MAILMAN. Oh, I understand. I get that all the time. You were just expecting someone else.

JENNY. Yeh. Kinda.

MAILMAN. Big man about—(*Indicates.*)—yea tall on a big white horse?

JENNY. (*Hopeful.*) Yeah, that's him. Seen him around?

MAILMAN. Not lately. Here, I need you to sign for this.

JENNY. Sign? Wow. Sure. A registered letter? For me? (*SHE signs.*)

MAILMAN. (*As HE goes.*) Have a nice day.

JENNY. (*As SHE rips the letter open.*) A registered letter that reeks of cologne.

(*SHE begins to read and LOVERBOY appears.*)

LOVERBOY. Oh baby, this is the twentieth letter I've started in my humble attempt to tell you how I feel. The appropriate words abandon me, but I fear if I wait much longer you will have forgotten me completely.

(*Break—JENNY reacts.*)

LOVERBOY. Forgive me for not calling, but I couldn't possibly express my feelings to you any way but through a letter. Cowardice perhaps, but the greatest of men are cowards when it comes to a beautiful woman.

(*Break—JENNY giggles.*)

LOVERBOY. Silly of me perhaps—again I say "perhaps;" am I overusing the word? Silly of me to dare to believe that a woman such as you would consider spending her life with me, although I must admit, I am very nice looking, you said so yourself. Although I'm sure you've heard all of this before from men perhaps worthier than I— I must dare to spill my heart and say I love you as I've loved no other. I know that we spent only that one night together, but I've relived that hour again and again. I ache to kiss your beautiful red lips—

JENNY. (*To audience.*) Beautiful red lips!

(*LOVERBOY freezes each time JENNY looks up to audience.*)

LOVERBOY. —and gaze into your beautiful blue eyes—

JENNY. Beautiful blue eyes!

LOVERBOY. —to run my fingers through your luscious silky black hair—

JENNY. Luscious silky black hair!

LOVERBOY. —and to caress your—

(*JENNY stops, looks up confused, and then rereads last sentence.*)

LOVERBOY. —through your luscious silky black hair—

JENNY. Luscious Silky *blonde* hair.

LOVERBOY. Silky *black* hair.

JENNY. Silky blonde hair!

LOVERBOY. Black hair!

JENNY. Blonde!
LOVERBOY. Black!
JENNY. Blonde!
LOVERBOY. Black!

(JENNY desperately grabs the envelope to check address.)

LOVERBOY. *(Backing up to his chair.)* Mary Davies, 42 Ashford Lane.

JENNY. *(To audience.)* Seeing the name sent venom through my veins. While just seconds before, while reading the letter intended for some tramp—us women like to refer to women who have what we want as tramps—not fair really—but it makes us feel better about ourselves. So ... while reading the letter intended for the tramp, I felt what it was like to be wanted—what it was like to *be* Mary Davies—and oh, it was a heavenly feeling. And in spite of the horrendous outcome of the letter, it triggered something in me—a want, an incredible want. And if you want it badly enough you can get it.

(As JOE steps center, GROUP begins bass sound—BUM-BUM-BUM-BUM-BUM—and continues throughout the following.)

JENNY. Joe was a bass man, the best, the very best, everybody thought so. We had performed in the same performance hall for over a year. I had probably even borrowed a pencil from him in comp class. I had heard his music but never associated the sound with the man. Until he's pointed out to you, you just don't notice him.

(GROUP ends bass sound.)

JENNY. His long drab coat hides his rather mysterious body. His little brown cap shades his piercing blue eyes. And his "You can't see me" attitude hides his heavy heart. Oh Joe, Joe, Joe, Joe, Joe. When he spoke his name so matter-of-factly, the first day of jazz ensemble, for the benefit of those who didn't know him—I was the only one—I noticed him—

(AMY, HENRY, CRYSTAL, POLLY, SEAN and DAVID step forward.)

HENRY. *(Arrogant.)* I'm Henry Michaels, as if you didn't know. We will be working together for the next six weeks. I have hopes of continuing our work together, but that will depend on you. You are all familiar with one another's work, I'm sure. There is no need to make introductions, is there? *(THE GROUP is silent.)* You truly don't know each other?
CRYSTAL. I know everybody. I've seen everybody before. I don't know everybody's name, but I know who everybody is. I know what instruments they play. I haven't talked to everybody personally. Basically, I have heard everybody play but I don't know what their fears are or what drives them as human beings—or animals for that matter. So as far as: "Do we know each other?" Does anybody really know anybody?
HENRY. Everyone, just say your name and your instrument.
CRYSTAL. Crystal. Not silver, or china, just Crystal. Oh ... piccolo.

AMY. Amy Jones. Trumpet.
JENNY. Jenny? Violin?
DAVID. David. Transferring to Julliard.
HENRY. Oh. Humor. Your instrument please.
DAVID. Oboe.
POLLY. Polly Fieldings. I, too, play violin.
JOE. Joe. Bass.
SEAN. Sean. Percussion.

(ACTION freezes as JENNY runs to the audience.)

JENNY. Listen! Did you hear that?

(The action goes back to Polly's line prior to Joe's.)

POLLY. Polly Fieldings. I, too, play violin.
JOE. Joe.
JENNY. Joe. *(SHE's thrilled.)*
JOE. Bass. *(HE moves toward her.)*
JENNY. Bass.
JOE. Joe.
JENNY. Joe.
JOE. Bass.
JENNY. Bass.
JOE. Joe!
JENNY. Joe!
JOE. Bass!

JENNY. Bass! Oh Joe Joe Joe Joe Joe Joe Joe.

(GROUP including JOE returns to upstage chairs.)

JENNY. I noticed him. And I noticed him some more. From that moment on I could not stop noticing him. But I had noticed men before.

(A handsome MAN WITH PAPER begins crossing the stage. JENNY continues speaking, but is more interested in watching the man.)

JENNY. And just because I noticed them—didn't mean they noticed—

(The MAN knocks JENNY over and drops his newspaper. JENNY grabs the paper and tugs on his shirt.)

JENNY. Oh—Hey, mister. You dropped your newspaper. Hey, mister, you dropped your newspaper.

(The MAN is oblivious to her. SOPHISTICATED LADY steps forward and takes paper from Jenny.)

SOPHISTICATED LADY. Excuse me, sir, I believe you dropped your newspaper.
MAN WITH PAPER. Oh, right you are. Please tell me you will accept an invitation to dinner at the restaurant of your choice as my humble way of saying thank you.
SOPHISTICATED LADY. I will accept your invitation to dinner at the restaurant of my choice as your humble way of saying thank you. I know just the place.

(THEY return to chairs, arm in arm, as JENNY watches dumbfounded.)

JENNY. But Joe was not an ordinary man. No, Joe was a man waiting for a woman to happen. Those two words: "Joe—Bass," told me his story. He needed me and I knew it. Now *he* just needed to know it. Beethoven was responsible for bringing this particular group together. Beethoven's 5th, transformed into Mr. Michaels' musical version of the sounds of New Orleans at the turn of the century, was the piece. Although I love Beethoven and his creation of the 5th, he neglected to provide me with a duet with Joe. So any getting to know Joe had to be during his breaks, while he was reading a book, smoking his camel non-filters, studying his notes, or polishing his instrument—

(JOE is sitting stage right reading. JENNY crosses to him.)

JENNY. Hi, Joe. Whatcha doin'? (*SHE smiles.*)
JOE. (*Without looking up.*) Readin'.
JENNY. Whatcha readin'?
JOE. *Cujo.*
JENNY. Is it a good book?
JOE. A very good book.
JENNY. Oh? What's it about?
JOE. A dog.
JENNY. What kind of dog?
JOE. (*Glances up.*) A rabid dog.
JENNY. Oh. What breed?
JOE. A St. Bernard.
JENNY. Is he a puppy or full grown? Or is he a she dog?

JOE. I'll let you read it when I'm through. Then you can find out for yourself.

JENNY. Oh, thanks, Joe. *(SHE runs to audience.)* Oh, Joe. Joe. Joe. Joe. Joe. Joe. Joe. I closed my eyes— *(Closes eyes.)*—put my mind on rewind—and played the conversation over again in my head. *(JENNY returns to him as before.)* Hi, Joe, whatcha doin'?

JOE. *(Stares wantonly at her.)* Lookin'.

JENNY. Whatcha looking at?

JOE. You—the prettiest girl I ever saw.

JENNY. *(Kneels before him. Sincere.)* Joe, did you know that when I was seven years old I fell upside down from a swing onto a pile of bricks? It bled, Joe. It bled bad. And did you know that ever since that day I've been able to see things and places that no one has ever seen before? I'll let you see them, Joe.

JOE. I'd go anywhere with you.

MAILMAN. *(Interrupts.)* Nice day, huh?

(JOE returns to his upstage chair.)

JENNY. A wonderful day. *(To audience.)* A day filled with Joe. *(To Mailman.)* Anything for me?

MAILMAN. *(Hands her three letters.)* Three for Mary Davies.

JENNY. *(Taking them.)* That's not me.

MAILMAN. Oh. *(Confused—digs through bag, finds one more.)* And one for ... Jenny Brown?

JENNY. Oh that's me! *(Takes it.)* Oh.

MAILMAN. You look disappointed.

JENNY. Yeah, I am a little disappointed. It's from my sister. Nothing against my sister—

MAILMAN. I understand. You were expecting something else.

JENNY. Yeah, kinda.

MAILMAN. A heart-shaped box about yea-big filled with chocolates?

JENNY: Yeah, that's it. Got one in your bag?

· MAILMAN. Nah, must've eaten it on the way (ha ha).

(Awkward pause.)

JENNY. *(Handing back Mary's letters.)* Oh, return these to sender, Tramp unknown.

MAILMAN. Popular girl.

JENNY. Yeah.

MAILMAN. See ya.

(JENNY opens letter. CHRISSY steps center.)

CHRISSY. *(Quickly.)* Dear Jenny. Eddie and I got caught sneaking out to elope. Dad now lets me see him if I promise not to marry him or let him in the house. I guess that's fair for now. Eddie thinks Dad thinks he won. I think it's nice to have food, clothing, and shelter. I do want to marry Eddie, but I think I should wait 'til I'm eighteen. He's a little jealous right now, 'cause two of his friends asked me out behind his back. And he got mad at me ... but I can't help what his friends do, right? I mean he'd probably be really mad at his friends if they didn't ask me out. He'd be scared that they didn't think I was attractive. I'm not worried about his friends, but there is a new guy in Chemistry who asked me for Saturday night. I don't want to go, but I don't want to hurt his feelings. God, I'm so confused and depressed. Love, Chrissy.

JENNY. (*Turns to chart #3 with pictures of what she is describing.*) The world is divided into: Those who have and like what they have; those who have but think they could have better; those who don't have and don't care; and those who don't have but want to have. And it's those women that have that the men that don't have want to have. So for all of the Chrissys in the world—shut up! Be happy! You have!

(JOE is sitting stage right tuning his bass.)

JENNY. Based on information from my chart, I knew it was important that I appear to be a haver, so I borrowed some male acquaintances and headed for Joe. (*SHE links arms with two men outside of her door and crosses by Joe.*) For the next two weeks I tried the "Look-at-me-I'm-such-a-together-happy-go-lucky-woman-who-doesn't-need-you" attitude.

(THEY strut by Joe.)

JENNY. But Joe never looked up to notice that I wasn't noticing him.

(CRYSTAL enters and crosses to Joe.)

JOE. Hey Crystal, do you have a minute to go over the third movement?

CRYSTAL. Sure thing, Joe, just let me freshen up.

(CRYSTAL and JOE touch. JENNY gasps in agony at the sight of this.)

CRYSTAL. God, Jenny, what's the matter? You sick?
JENNY. I hate him.
CRYSTAL. Who? Joe? You hate Joe? Why?
JENNY. I just hate him.
CRYSTAL. Hate's a very strong word, Jenny. What'd he do to you?
JENNY. Absolutely nothing.
CRYSTAL. Oh, you mean you like him. Oh, Jenny, you could do better than Joe.
JENNY. Hey, it doesn't get any better than Joe.
CRYSTAL. Don't get me wrong, Jenny, I think he's a great musician. But just look at him. Look at his eyes. There's something evil. I heard he's into devil worship— *(THEY stare at him.)*—I could be wrong.
JENNY. Of course you're wrong.
CRYSTAL. Why do you like him?
JENNY. Why do pigs like mud?
CRYSTAL. *(Taking question seriously.)* Because they have dry skin, and the mud cools them off. Pigs are actually very neat creatures. It's a funny thing about pigs, they have a reputation for being dirty but sweet, when they're actually clean and nasty. The cow's reputation is also inaccurate, they—
JENNY. Crystal, how do you know so much about farm animals?
CRYSTAL. I dated a farmer when I was in Oklahoma, so I made a point of understanding the animals. And when I dated a philosophy professor, I read up on philosophy. And

now that I'm dating a dentist, I know a lot about teeth.
(*Smiles.*)

JENNY. What's the longest you've been without a
relationship?

CRYSTAL. Actually, they tend to overlap. It always
seems to work out that—

JENNY. Oh you're just one of those have people, aren't
you?! You've always been a haver, haven't you? You're a
haver! You're a haver!

CRYSTAL. Jenny! That's a terrible thing to say to me.
I would never say anything like that to you. That really
hurts. You know you've really changed. I thought you
were—

JENNY. Yeah—well—I'm sorry. Sometimes it's
important, though, that people know how others see them.
I hate to be the one to tell you, but you're a haver—
everybody thinks so.

JOE. (*Calls out to Crystal.*) Hey, Crystal—

CRYSTAL. In a second, Joe. (*To Jenny.*) That hurt
Jenny. That really hurt.

(*CRYSTAL goes to Joe and the TWO return to their
    chairs.*)

JENNY. (*To audience.*) I hated Crystal. Actually I hated
in Crystal what I lacked in myself. I liked Crystal. I wanted
to be like Crystal. I wanted that direct connection from my
brain to my mouth leaving no time for editing thoughts.
She just said things—smart things and stupid things—but
people at least looked at her when she talked. And Crystal
got results. What was important to her men was important
to her. So I—

MAILMAN. Hi, Jenny.

JENNY. (*Excited.*) Oh great! Is *that* what I think it is?

MAILMAN. (*With small box in hand.*) You look excited.

JENNY. I am excited.

MAILMAN. But it's not heart-shaped.

JENNY. It's better than candy, it's a book!

MAILMAN. So you're a book lover. (*Sees the book is Cujo.*) Oh—and a dog lover.

JENNY. Oh you've read it?

MAILMAN. Yeah.

JENNY. What'd you think?

MAILMAN. Well, it starts out—

JENNY. No—don't tell me. Thanks.

MAILMAN. Enjoy. (*HE goes.*)

(*JENNY opens to the first page and AUTHOR comes center. HE recites the lines as JENNY turns pages of the book.*)

AUTHOR. This book is for my brother David, who held my hand—(*Page flip/no pauses.*)—Not so long ago, a monster came to the small town. He killed a waitress named Alma—(*Page flip.*) Cujo sat up, and Gary saw a large ugly-looking scratch healing on the dog's muzzle—(*Page flip.*) MOMMY MOMMY MOMMY! (*Break—rereads same page.*) MOMMY MOMMY MOMMY! (*Flip.*) It's snapping jaws were inches from the bare flesh of (*Flip.*) He turned to find—(*Flip.*) zigzag (*Flip.*) hell (*Flip.*) die (*Flip.*) croak (*Fast flips:*)—big—blood—sane—

can—help—mommy—go—hey—the—(*Last page.*) The dog was rabid!*

(*JENNY slams the book shut and AUTHOR vanishes. It was a spiritual experience for Jenny. POLLY approaches.*)

POLLY. Hey, Jenny, Mr. Michaels said you could use some help with your solo. I've got some time if—
JENNY. (*More interested in* Cujo.) Oh my solo is fine.
POLLY. Don't get me wrong, but Mr. Michaels is concerned, and I'd hate to see—
JENNY. (*Sincerely.*) Do you want my solo? Is that it? You can have it. Really. Solo's are very lonely things.
POLLY. Jenny, I don't want your solo. I was just trying to help. (*POLLY starts to leave.*)
JENNY. Hey, Polly?
POLLY Yes?
JENNY. Do you have a boyfriend?
POLLY (*Pause.*) Yes.
JENNY. (*Pause.*) Really?
POLLY (*Pause.*) Yes.
JENNY. (*Pause.*) For a long time?
POLLY (*Pause.*) Yes.
JENNY. (*Pause.*) Hunh.

(*POLLY crosses to the others.*)

JENNY. Time passed and I took my studies very seriously. *Cujo* was more than a book about a rabid St.

---

*Used with permission. Stephen King, *Cujo* © 1981. All rights reserved.

Bernard who rips to shreds those he once loved—it was a story about love and pain. And after reading the text four times—I felt on solid footing—Joe and I now had common ground. I had earned my right to speak.

(JENNY runs toward JOE who is now sitting in a chair polishing his instrument.)

JENNY. Hey, Joe, you were so right about this book— *(JENNY falls into Joe's lap.)* Oh I'm so sorry.
    JOE. Why be sorry?
    JENNY. I didn't hurt your instrument did I?
    JOE. Not at all.
    JENNY. Oh good.
    JOE. I see you're reading *Cujo.* You have excellent taste. I see it as one of the greatest love stories of our time. A story of love and pain.
    JENNY. The pain of being driven by a passion that has diseased your spirit.
    JOE. Finally, a woman who understands great literature. A woman who understands me.
    JENNY. Joe?
    JOE. Yes?
    JENNY. Did you know that when I was seven years old, I fell—

(JOE kisses her on the cheek. CRYSTAL stands.)

    CRYSTAL. Hey, Joe, I'm ready.

(JOE leaps from the chair. JENNY lands on the floor.)

JENNY. He kissed me—at least I think it was a kiss. But it all happened so quickly, I couldn't be sure—

(JOE and CRYSTAL freeze.)

JENNY. —so I closed my eyes—*(Closes eyes.)*, put my mind on rewind *(CRYSTAL sits.)*—and played back the facts. *(Runs toward Joe as before.)* Hey Joe, you were so right about this book—*(SHE falls on him as before.)*
JOE. OW!
JENNY. I'm sorry. I didn't hurt—
CRYSTAL. Hey, Joe—

(JOE leaps up. JENNY falls. JOE spits at her as if her hair is in his mouth.)

JENNY. *(Thrilled.)* Yes, I felt a coolness on my cheek. So he kissed me on the cheek! Or he wiped his lips on my face—or he spit at me. My God, he spit at me! So he spit at me. Men have spit at me before.

(The MEN rise in unison, preparing to spit.)

JENNY. *(Turning on them:)* Oh, STOP!

(The MEN freeze then sit)

JENNY. Oh, I was all confused and losing hope. *(She is greeted by the MAILMAN.)*
MAILMAN. Hi there.
JENNY. Oh, hi.
MAILMAN. You look all confused and losing hope.

JENNY. What?

MAILMAN. You look all confused and losing hope.

JENNY. I am all confused and losing hope.

MAILMAN. (*Seeing book.*) So, how'd you like *Cujo*?

JENNY. (*Bitterly.*) Frightening.

MAILMAN. Yeah, that's what I thought.

JENNY. (*Tenderly.*) And very sad.

MAILMAN. You know, if you like dogs so much you really should read *Old Yeller*. It's not nearly as violent, and it's—

JENNY. (*Taking letters from him.*) Yeah, I'll think about it.

MAILMAN. Take care of yourself. (*HE goes.*)

JENNY. (*Joyously to audience.*) When there's mail, there's hope!

(*JENNY opens first envelope and as SHE reads TELEPHONE WOMAN appears upstage.*)

TELEPHONE WOMAN. Dear Ms. Brown 555-1432. Have you forgotten something? This notice is to inform you that your balance is past due. Unless payment of $165.88 is received—

(*JENNY violently rips letter. With each specific rip, TELEPHONE WOMAN screams and physically reacts. JENNY crumples torn pieces and tosses them aside, sending TELEPHONE WOMAN back to chairs. JENNY opens second letter and a MILITARY MAN appears.*)

MILITARY MAN. Dear Ms. Brown, Jenny. Have you always wanted to travel to exotic countries? Have you always wanted the opportunity to serve your country but weren't sure how? The United States Armed Forces are looking for—

(JENNY crumples letter, violently smashing it between her hands—throws it on the ground—stomps on it several times—twists it into the floor with her foot, then kicks it offstage. MILITARY MAN reacts accordingly, falling to the floor, feeling the stomps etc. and flies back to seat when it is kicked off.)

JENNY. The mail offered no solution. *(Returning to chart #3.)* I decided to return to my chart and try to figure out what the havers had—aside from having each other—that I didn't have. Then it hit me. My God, what was I thinking—of course Joe wasn't going to like me—Look at my thighs—I have no tone. And then I heard these voices—

GROUP. GET THEE TO A HEALTH SPA. GET THEE TO A HEALTH SPA.

(AMY and CRYSTAL join JENNY down center and begin stretching in unison to MUSIC. INSTRUCTOR stands on the bench leading the aerobics class. JOE is upstage doing his own workout.)

JENNY. *(Seeing Joe through her legs.)* Oh my God, Joe's here.

CRYSTAL. Ignore him.

INSTRUCTOR. Backs flat, ladies, and one ...

(CRYSTAL, AMY and JENNY do synchronized exercises, giving it their all.)

JENNY. God, why is he making this so hard? What's wrong with me?

AMY. It's not you. It's the rating system. On a scale of 1 to 10, how would you rate Joe?

JENNY. A 10.

CRYSTAL. A 10?!

INSTRUCTOR. Back shoulder isolations.

AMY. Keep in mind that men aren't rated on looks, they're rated on power and position. Although Joe has incredible potential, he has no money, no car, no Pulitzer Prizes—he couldn't possibly be a 10.

CRYSTAL. Give him a 6.

INSTRUCTOR. Now front.

AMY. How would you rate yourself?

JENNY. A 6.

CRYSTAL. Oh, you're at least a 7.5.

JENNY. *(Pleased.)* Really?

AMY. Let's just say Jenny's a 7 and Joe's a 6. One would think that Joe the 6, would be flattered to be with Jenny the 7, right?

JENNY. Right.

AMY. Wrong. A 6 wants a ...

CRYSTAL ... 6, so he doesn't have to feel inferior.

AMY. Wrong. A 6 wants a 10. And a 10 wants a ...

JENNY & CRYSTAL. 10.

AMY. And a 2 wants ...

JENNY & CRYSTAL. a 10.

AMY. Everyone wants a ...

JENNY, CRYSTAL, AMY. TEN!!!

CRYSTAL. That is so negative.

INSTRUCTOR. Ready for aerobics! And kick and—

AMY. But there are ways to beat the system. Depending on the angle from which you are being judged, you can get bonus points. A 20-year-old 6 being viewed by an old man automatically becomes at least a 9 based on her youth alone. Hopefully she knows the value of her youth, and doesn't sell it just for points. And, then there's always money—a rich woman being viewed by a poor man. Compassion. Success. Humor. And of course, love. Love adds five points to any woman's face. So the difference between acquiring points versus having them at the get go, equals the difference between growing on someone versus having someone fall for you. For example, Crystal is a fall-for, and I'm a grow-on.

JENNY. My God! This would make an incredible chart!

INSTRUCTOR. And scissors! And one—

CRYSTAL. So what are you saying Jenny is?

AMY. Well, obviously with Joe, she's a grow-on.

JENNY. (*Horrified.*) I'm a grow-on?!

AMY. What'd you think you were, a fall-for?

JENNY. No, but isn't there something else? Do I have to be a grow-on?

AMY. You say that as if it's some kind of disease. I'm a grow-on.

JENNY. Well, maybe you like being one. I don't want to be one, makes me feel like a growth, like some kind of wart. I'm not a wart, I'm a woman—

AMY. I'm hardly a wart, Jenny!

CRYSTAL. I don't think either one of you are—

JENNY. Oh, what do you know—you're a fall-for haver!

INSTRUCTOR. And bring it on home!

(THEY begin frantically running in place.)

AMY. Hey, I *earned* my status! And I never have to worry about my husband slipping away when I get older, because I grew all over him, and he grew all over me—our roots are completely intertwined.

CRYSTAL. That's beautiful!

AMY. It is! (*Still madly running in place.*)

JENNY. The fact is—I would be more than happy to grow on Joe and I've tried—but he's so slippery or something—there's nothing to attach myself to.

AMY. He has to notice you first.

CRYSTAL. Yeah, send out signals.

JENNY. I have.

CRYSTAL. Hit him over the head.

JENNY. (*Stops running.*) With what?!

AMY. With everything you've got. You just hit him over the head.

CRYSTAL. Hit him over the head.

AMY. Hit him over the head.

CRYSTAL. Hit him over the head.

AMY. Hit him over the head.

GROUP. (*ALL join in chanting.*) Hit him over the head! Hit him over the head!

JENNY. (*Breaks away. To audience.*) They were right. Perhaps my signals had been somewhat subtle. Besides, I feared they were about to break into song.

(JENNY crosses to JOE who is working out with free weights. SHE slips along side him and matches his exercises.)

JENNY. Hey, Joe?
JOE. Yepper.
JENNY. *(To audience, whisper.)* Yepper? *(To Joe.)* You toning up?
JOE. Yepper.
JENNY. *(To audience, whisper.)* Yepper? *(To Joe.)* You sweat much?
JOE. Yep.
JENNY. Hey, Joe?
JOE. Yepper.
JENNY. I like you.
JOE. Yepper.
JENNY. Do you like me?
JOE. Yep.
JENNY. *(Thrilled.)* Wow—Really, Joe?
JOE. Yepper.
JENNY. You're not just saying that?
JOE. Yepper.
JENNY. Wow.
JOE. Yep.
JENNY. Wait—Yepper you are just saying that—
JOE. Yepper.
JENNY. —or yepper you're not?
JOE. Yepper.
JENNY. Well—which one is it?
JOE. Yep.
JENNY. *(To the audience—disgusted and frustrated.)* How do you talk to a "yepper" and what does "yepper"

mean? So I didn't understand him—but I had not
understood men before.

(PIERRE steps forward.)

PIERRE. *Oh, vous êtes tres belle! Étes vous ici pour
moi?*
JENNY. What?
PIERRE. *Oh vous êtes tres belle! Étes vous ici pour
moi?*
JENNY. Sorry, what?

(A FRENCH WOMAN enters and overhears him.)

PIERRE. *Oh vous êtes tres belle! Étes vous ici pour
moi?*
MICHELLE. *(Approaches Pierre.)* Ah! Je m'appelle
Michelle. Je t'aime.

(THEY kiss passionately and return to chairs.)

JENNY. So I didn't speak Joe's language. But
somebody out there did. *(SEAN walks by.)* Sean?
SEAN. Yep?
JENNY. *(A smile of success from JENNY.)* You're a
guy.
SEAN. Yep, I like to think so.
JENNY. Well as a guy, have you ever had a—you
know, communication barrier between you and a woman
you were interested in where you were trying to tell her
how much you liked her but she didn't speak your language

and misinterpreted all of your come-ons as just little grunts
of tolerance at her existence?
SEAN and MEN. Sure, every guy has.

*(The MEN and WOMEN still seated along the upstage wall
take part in the conversation.)*

JENNY. Yeah?
SEAN and MEN. Sure.
JENNY. Even Joe?
SEAN. Joe?!
GROUP MEMBER #1. (*Overlapping.*) Joe?!
GROUP MEMBER #2. (*Overlapping.*) Joe?!
GROUP MEMBER #3. (*Overlapping.*) Joe?!
GROUP MEMBER #4. (*Overlapping.*) Joe?!
GROUP MEMBER #5. (*Overlapping.*) Joe?!
SEAN. Oh Jenny, Joe?!
GROUP MEMBER #1. (*Overlapping.*) Oh, Jenny, Joe?!
GROUP MEMBER #2. (*Overlapping.*) Oh, Jenny,
Joe?!
GROUP MEMBER #3. (*Overlapping.*) Oh, Jenny,
Joe?!
GROUP MEMBER #4. (*Overlapping.*) Oh, Jenny,
Joe?!
GROUP MEMBER #5. (*Overlapping.*) Oh, Jenny,
Joe?!
SEAN and GROUP. You like Joe?!
JENNY. (*Embarrassed.*) Just a little.
SEAN. Ya know, Joe reminds me of this woman I used
to know—Melissa. Wouldn't give me the time of day. I
couldn't figure the snob out, then I find out from a friend
of hers, that Melissa was absolutely terrified—

*(MELISSA stands, lets out a BLOOD-CURDLING
    SCREAM. Sits.)*

   SEAN. —of men.
   JENNY. Terrified?
   SEAN Terrified!

(MELISSA stands, screams, and sits.)

   JENNY. My God! That's awful!
   SEAN. Hey, a lot of women are terrified—

(ALL the WOMEN stand and SCREAM!)

   SEAN. —of men.
   JENNY. *(Are you sure?)* Terrified?
   SEAN. You know ... scared.

(The WOMEN stand, let out a smaller scream.)

   JENNY. Oh.
   SEAN. Very uncomfortable.

(The WOMEN squirm with a whimper of discomfort.)

   JENNY. Oh.
   SEAN. And rightfully so. There are a lot of guys out
there you just can't trust.
   JENNY. And you think Joe's one of them?
   SEAN. No. I think that maybe, similar to Melissa,
Joe's terrified—

(JOE stands and screams, surprising even himself.)

SEAN. —of women.
JENNY. Wow!

(JOE feels humiliated by having to do this, shoots a look to Jenny and Sean, then sits.)

SEAN. 'Cause there's a lot of women out there you can't trust either.
JENNY. Joe can trust me.
SEAN. Well, let him know—let him know you care.
JENNY. Is that what you did with Melissa?
SEAN. No—'cause I didn't.

(The GROUP enters with MR. MICHAELS. In a bar. THEY form a loose semi-circle. JENNY stands opposite of JOE.)

HENRY. You were all terrible tonight. What happened to everyone? There was no music tonight—just noise—sounds. We exist to make music—MUSIC.
SEAN. Aren't we allowed one bad rehearsal?
HENRY. One bad rehearsal? This was not bad—this was frightening.
DAVID. Beethoven's 5th transformed to the sounds of New Orleans at the turn of the century is frightening.
HENRY. You say you want to be professionals? Well professionals aren't afraid to do something new—something that hasn't already been done. What's happening? Nobody's committing to the music. We're

trying something new here. To accomplish this we must
focus. You can't be afraid to go for it.

*(JENNY leaps forward as SHE shouts out. ALL freeze
    except for JOE.)*

JENNY. Joe, wanna dance?
JOE. *(Stepping forward.)* I thought you'd never ask.
JENNY. Oh but the music has stopped.
JOE. We can dance to the music of our hearts.

(BOTH quickly step back. GROUP returns to normal.)

HENRY. *(As before.)* You were all selected by me
because I knew you had it in you. I knew you had the
ability, the dedication and the guts. Prove to me you still
have guts!
JENNY. *(Leaps forward.)* Joe!
JOE. *(Steps out.)* Jenny! Jenny will you marry me?
JENNY. Couldn't we live together first? *(Back to
normal.)*
HENRY. *(As before.)* We have exactly one week to
clean this up. And Jenny I expect you to put in overtime.
Your solo sounds like garbage—
POLLY. I've offered to help her but she—
HENRY. Not now, sweetheart. When I originally
planned to bring you all here, I intended this to be a semi-
celebration—
JENNY. *(Jumps forward.)* JOE!

*(JOE does not join her in her fantasy and JENNY is alone
    in the center of the semi-circle. This is reality. All is*

*quiet and EVERYONE stares. SHE is mortified and
steps backward into the group, her head hung low.)*

HENRY. —a positive reinforcement of the work you
had accomplished. But, now, I don't think I can stay—I'm
saddened and I'm hurt by what I've witnessed tonight.
(*HENRY goes.*)

POLLY. Poor Mr. Michaels.

DAVID. I can't believe he's blaming us for his
incompetence. A man completely destroys one of history's
great musical accomplishments and he hates you for
knowing how horrendous it is.

JENNY. Oh my God! What have I done?

POLLY. I can still help you with your solo if—

JENNY. Oh I don't care about my solo, Polly! I
want—

*(The GROUP is returning to their chairs. CRYSTAL and
AMY huddle with JENNY. JOE crosses center.)*

AMY. If you're going to do anything about it, now's
the time. He's very vulnerable after a bad rehearsal.

CRYSTAL. Just keep hitting him over the head with
it.

AMY. (*Pushing JENNY toward Joe.*) Hit him over the
head.

JENNY. (*With Joe.*) Joe. Wanna dance?

JOE. There isn't any music.

JENNY. I thought we could dance to the music of our
h—(*Runs back to Amy and Crystal.*)

AMY. What happened?

JENNY. He didn't want to dance.

AMY. He wouldn't dance with you?

CRYSTAL. But there isn't any music.

JENNY. Well I didn't mean tonight. I didn't say—Joe wanna dance TONIGHT. I just said, Joe, would you like to dance; if he misinterpreted, that's his problem.

AMY. Don't give up now. He looks like a man in need of some liquid refreshment. (*SHE pushes Jenny.*)

JENNY. Joe, can I buy you a liquid?

JOE. A liquid?

JENNY. A beer or something?

JOE. A beer would be great.

(*JENNY goes to Amy and Crystal.*)

CRYSTAL. What'd he say?

JENNY. (*Excited.*) A beer, he wants a beer.

AMY. Go ahead back. I'll get it.

JENNY. Oh, I'm scared.

CRYSTAL. (*Pushing her.*) You're doing great.

JENNY. (*Back with Joe.*) A beer's on it's way.

AMY. (*With beer in hand.*) I didn't know what kind, so—

JENNY. (*Grabbing beer.*) This is fine.

JOE. Amy, do you want to join us?

JENNY. Why?!!!—

AMY. (*A little thrown by Jenny's behavior.*) No. Thanks. (*Returns to Crystal.*)

JENNY. How's your beer? Is it okay?

JOE. Yep, it's very good.

JENNY. Thanks.

JOE. Aren't you having one?

JENNY. No, I'll just watch you.

(Pause.
During the following, whenever Jenny's at a loss for
words, SHE turns to AMY and CRYSTAL who feed
her lines from stage right. Full voice.)

JENNY. Amy told me you were a—
AMY. A cancer.
JENNY. A cancer.
JOE. Yep.
JENNY. That's great.
JOE. Why?
JENNY. Well—
CRYSTAL. I'm an Aquarius.
JENNY. Crystal's an Aquarius.
AMY. No, you're an Aquarius.
JENNY. No, you're an Aquarius. No. I'm an Aquarius.
JOE. So—
JENNY. So—
AMY. They have a lot in common.
JENNY. They have a lot in common.
JOE. Like what?
JENNY. They both like—
AMY. Good books—
JENNY. Good books—
JOE. As opposed to bad books?
JENNY. Yeah, and they both like—
CRYSTAL. Candlelight dinners.
JENNY. Candlelight dinners.
JOE. Do you follow that stuff?
JENNY. Not really. *(Pause.)* So—
CRYSTAL and AMY. Joe—

JENNY. Joe—
CRYSTAL. Are you really—
JENNY. Are you really—
CRYSTAL. Into devil worship?
JENNY. Into devil worship? (*Panicked—shoots a look at Crystal.*)
AMY. —In the mood for a home-cooked meal—
JENNY. —In the mood for a home-cooked meal—
CRYSTAL. by candlelight—
JENNY. by candlelight—
JOE. Sure. When?
CRYSTAL. Ooo, let's say—
JENNY. Ooo, let's say—
AMY. 8:30 on the 13th?
JENNY. 8:30 on the 13th?
JOE. That should be fine.
JENNY. Oh. Do you need my address?
JOE. No. It's Mary Davies' old apartment, isn't it?
JENNY. Yeh.
JOE. (*Finishes beer.*) So the 13th—I'll mark it down. (*JOE looks her straight in the eye—a quick smile or touch—then exits bar area.*)
JENNY. (*Thrilled. To Crystal and Amy.*) How'd I sound?
CRYSTAL and AMY. Very natural.
JENNY. (*To the audience.*) Oh yes, Joe. I wanted Joe. I was in like with—love with—crushed on Joe. Yes, Joe. (*Running home.*) I'll cook and clean and light my candles for you and only you. (*Begins madly cleaning her apartment—excitement building.*) I cooked and cleaned and cleaned and cooked all day. I spent ten dollars on perfumed candles. I cleaned and cooked some more. Wednesday night

came—(*Excitement peaks and breaks.*)—but Joe didn't. A simple phone call ... a simple lie: "I've been shot." Even a "Look, bitch, I think you're ugly and couldn't stomach the idea of sitting across from you over dinner so I'm standing you up." But this silent kind of rejection. This rejectionless rejection. This "there still may be hope, he might really be lost" rejection—It was too much to take. (*Leaving her apartment with notebook in hand.*) So I decided to walk an hour or two to the corner bar and write a letter to my mother to apologize for all the times I fed my dinner to the dog.

(*A LOUNGE SINGER and the ACCOMPANIST cross to piano as JENNY takes a slow melancholy cross in step with the MUSIC.*)
LOUNGE SINGER sings a love song about a man named Joe.
JENNY shoots a look at singer on the final note of "Joe" and sits. MAN IN BAR sits two seats from her.)

LOUNGE SINGER. Thank you. Thank you. Back in ten.

(*JENNY writes. MAN IN BAR watches her. BARTENDER approaches.*)

BARTENDER. And what's the pretty little lady drinking tonight?

(*JENNY goes on writing.*)

BARTENDER. I said, what can I get for the pretty little lady? (*Nudging her.*) What'll you have?

JENNY. Oh uh, Bloody Mary ... Davies.

(*BARTENDER gets the drink as JENNY continues writing. MAN IN BAR inches closer.*)

MAN IN BAR. Hey, are you a writer?

JENNY. Excuse me?

MAN IN BAR. Oh, I'm sorry—don't let me bother you.

JENNY. No, what?

MAN IN BAR. Nothing. (*Little laugh.*)

JENNY. (*Little laugh.*) No, really, what?

MAN IN BAR. No, really, it was nothing.

JENNY. (*Laughing.*) Oh, come on.

MAN IN BAR. Naahhh.

JENNY. Oh, pleeeaaase.

MAN IN BAR. (*Firm.*) No.

JENNY. (*Sober.*) Okay. (*JENNY returns to writing. Finally:*)

MAN IN BAR. I just thought that maybe you were one of those women who is so uptight in a bar that she has to pretend to be studying or somethin'—some kind of complex where she doesn't feel justified as a human being, and feels it is below her to make it known in public that she suffers from occasional loneliness just like everyone else. But see to her—her loneliness has become so—

JENNY. —magnified—

MAN IN BAR. No—magnified—in her own head that she honestly believes no one else has ever felt such a—

JENNY. —hollow—

MAN IN BAR. No—hollow feeling. She imagines that everyone is studying her every move.

(JENNY turns to see Group. GROUP grins. SHE turns away and grabs her drink.)

MAN IN BAR. She can't even sip from her drink without fearing that people will recognize that she is drinking it out of need rather than a simple ordinary middle class thirst that alcohol often quenches.

(SHE puts her drink down, defeated. As SHE reaches to brush back her hair:)

MAN IN BAR. And she can't brush a piece of hair out of her eyes without fearing that people will misread her innocent act as vanity—

(A little shake of the head trying to move hair.)

MAN IN BAR. —or some kind of signal to the members of the opposite sex that she is on the make—

(JENNY blows hair.)

MAN IN BAR. —ready for a roll—

(Blows.)

MAN IN BAR. —eager to please.

(Big blow.)

MAN IN BAR. That misplaced hair hangs hour after hour before she finally gets enough nerve to take that lonely walk to the bathroom. That dreadful, silent, awkward, clumsy walk.

(JENNY is completely entranced by now, feeling all he is saying.)

MAN IN BAR. At first she is comforted by the confusion of the crowd, but halfway from her stool to the bathroom door, all is quiet. Her lonely blue aura begins glowing intensely. All eyes on her. It's too late to turn back. She finds something interesting to focus on: the sign to the ladies room, the "We have the right to refuse service to anyone we please" notice. She attempts to combat her fears by pausing briefly under the sign and feigning great interest. "I am not afraid," she convinces herself. But she feels the eyes on her back. She knows they are staring at her panty lines. Finally she takes another step toward her destination—then two giant leaps. She takes refuge in the rest room—sobs into the mirror, "Why am I such a freak?!" She pounds the glass! "Why oh why can't I be like everybody else?"
JENNY. WHY?!
MAN IN BAR. And she is never seen again. A notebook of doodles is found under the barstool. Much like Cinderella's slipper. And the man who speaks her language, who understands her pains will search in vain for the woman who could not see herself as the ordinary but beautiful female she really was.

JENNY. (*In awe.*) How do you know so much about those women?

MAN IN BAR. I used to be one of those women.

(*JENNY is speechless as the MAN stands up.*)

MAN IN BAR. But, hey, I didn't want to interrupt. I'll let you get back to your work.

(*MAN IN BAR heads back to his upstage chair. A subtle tug at his panty line.*
LOUNGE SINGER—reprise of first song from his chair, a capella.
JENNY drinks down her Bloody Mary during reprise. SHE then rises, takes a step—a BLUE LIGHT FLICKERS over her head. SHE stops, then bravely attempts the long walk out of the bar. GROUP stares. JENNY stops twice, turning to catch them staring, but THEY all turn away in time. The third head turn, SHE catches them.)

JENNY. (*Shouting.*) WHAT ARE YOU ALL STARING AT?!

GROUP. Nothin'.

(*BLUE LIGHT out.*)

JENNY. (*To audience.*) All right, so I felt like nothin'. Joe stood me up. I didn't know why and I didn't know if knowing why would really help. To question Joe on the matter, only to discover that he was out with another woman—or worse yet, just plain home watching TV— would be cementing me into the loser position and admitting that he won. So keeping quiet and assuming the worst—that he had no excuse—protected me from furthering my embarrassment and humiliation. I decided to take my friends' advice about Joe and just—

GROUP. Forget him.

JENNY. (*To audience.*) Yes it was time to move forward—time to close the chapter on Joe and reunite with my first true love: my violin. But my ego was suffering just miserably. It needed to know that he did have an excuse—a damned good excuse—maybe he had an embarrassing illness—and the only reason he hadn't told me of it already was to save face in front of me—the only woman he truly loved. (*SHE gets a rose.*) Besides, what harm is there in one little innocent rose sent anonymously by one little innocent woman. (*SHE hands the rose to MAILMAN.*)

MAILMAN. But, you need a box or something. You can't just send a rose—

JENNY. Just stick a stamp on it.

MAILMAN. Who shall I say it's from?

JENNY. If he loves me, he'll know who it's from—(*To audience.*)—and he'll admire my ability to forgive without interrogation.

MAILMAN. And if he doesn't love you?

JENNY. Bite your tongue! (*JENNY turns toward apartment.*)

MAILMAN. Wait. Your mail.

JENNY. Oh, thanks.

CHRISSY. (*Comes forward.*) Dear Jenny, when Eddie stood me up when we first started dating, I refused to talk to him for a week. Then he wrote me a poem:

EDDIE. (*Comes forward and recites poem.*)

I understand why you're upset with me
I have behaved very bad-ly
All I want is to apologize
and not try to fool you with stupid lies.
I was not stuck in traffic
or stuck sick in bed
The date of our meeting had just left my head.
I had been practicing getting you out of my mind
In case you didn't like me and left me behind.
So all I want is another chance—
to get into your underpants.

(EDDIE returns to his seat. CHRISSY continues.)

CHRISSY. Wasn't that sweet? See, Dad doesn't take the time to get to know the other sides of Eddie. I bet Dad never wrote Mom a poem. Anyway, gotta go. Not really—but I'm ending the letter anyway. Love you, miss you. Chrissy. *(CHRISSY returns to her seat.)*
JENNY. I awaited my Joe poem and his apology rose. But nothing. Opening night came and—

(JENNY crosses stage right to the dressing room where AMY and CRYSTAL are primping.)

AMY. Still no explanation from Joe?
JENNY. He threw my flower away. I saw it in the garbage.
AMY. That's terrible.
CRYSTAL. Maybe it was part of some ritual. Or maybe he simply didn't know what to do with it. A lot of

men have never received a flower. I can see how it could confuse them.

JENNY. I didn't send a card so I'm just pretending I didn't send it.

CRYSTAL. I think you should tell him that you sent it.

DAVID. (*Entering.*) I can't believe we have to go through with this. Wow, who got all the flowers?

CRYSTAL. Well most of these over here are mine including the long-stemmed red roses. The carnations are Amy's, the cactus is Polly's and the daisy is Jenny's.

JENNY. The daisy is mine? The daisy is mine? (*SHE runs to the huge mutant-sized daisy and searches for a card.*)

DAVID. Polly got a cactus? That's so cruel.

POLLY. (*Entering.*) There's nothing cruel about it. Gregory always sends a cactus. He's special. He loves me.

DAVID. Congratulations.

JENNY. You guys, there's no card. How do you know it's for me?

CRYSTAL. There was a card—

JENNY. (*Finding card.*) "JENNY." It's not signed. Just "JENNY."—OOHHHH, that's so Joe! Oh Wow!

HENRY. (*Enters. HE is nervous but peppy.*) They're going to love it. Trust me. Trust me. Oh, and Jenny, about your solo. It's not your solo. It's Polly's solo.

POLLY. Jenny, I'm sincerely sorry. But, I did try to—

JENNY. It's okay Polly, really.

HENRY. All right. Just play your hearts out. Relax, but with proper tension. Remember everything I told you. I've waited years for this. Big party afterwards. But for now, concentrate. Concentrate. Now get out there and go for it.

(The GROUP members take their positions center, facing HENRY who is conducting off the apron facing upstage.)

JENNY. *(To Joe.)* Thanks, Joe.
JOE. For what?
JENNY. The daisy.
JOE. Oh sure. What daisy?
JENNY. THE daisy.
JOE. Sorry. I don't know anything about a daisy.

(POLLY nudges Jenny from the soloist's center position.)

JENNY. *(To audience.)* He meant it. I could feel it. I thought I felt my heart crack—

(All the MUSICIANS, serious and prepared to play, watch for Henry's cue. HENRY begins conducting proudly. A strange version of Beethoven's 5th is heard. It sounds awful. We then reach POLLY's solo which is terribly hard on the ear. The piece is finished. GROUP bows slowly and apologetically while HENRY bows passionately. One by one THEY follow each other off, shooting looks of disgust at Henry.)

HENRY. *(To each as they pass.)* They loved it. They are stunned by its brilliance. You were all terrific. They really did like it. They hated it, didn't they? I'm sooo sorry. Oh God, I'm sorry. *(Grabs Joe and shakes him.)* My God, what was I thinking? Why did you let me do it? Why didn't somebody stop me? (*HENRY MICHAELS is a broken man.*)

JENNY. The show was over. The ensemble was history. Beethoven could once again rest in peace. I dragged myself to the party—carrying the daisy that Joe didn't send me. Finally, the daisy got to heavy too hold. (*JENNY drops the daisy with a thud.*)

(*Center stage becomes a party atmosphere. As JENNY enters the party area, the GROUP breaks into song— singing to the sounds of Beethoven's Fifth.*)

GROUP. (*Singing.*)
It's your birthdaaaaaaaaaay!
It's your birthdaaaaaaaaaay!
It's your birthday—it's your birthday—it's your birthday.
Your birthday—your birthday—your birthday.
Jenny's biiiiiirthdaaay!
Jenny's biiiiiirthdaaay!
Happy bi-irth —daaaaaaaaay!
JENNY. (*Excited.*). Wow. I didn't know you knew.

(*CRYSTAL and AMY approach Jenny.*)

CRYSTAL. Joe's in the bathroom. He'll probably—
JENNY. Joe? Who's Joe? Oh you mean Joe, that guy I liked yesterday when I was younger?
AMY. Maybe he prefers older women.
CRYSTAL. Maybe he won't date fellow musicians.
JENNY. And maybe I'm completely over him. (*To the audience.*) So Joe didn't sing to me on my birthday. So

lots of men have never sung to me on my birthday. So Joe was in the bathroom. But we had to get our beer from the same place, so it was inevitable that we—

JOE. Hey, Jenny. Happy—

JENNY. Where were you?!

JOE. In the bathroom.

JENNY. I mean Wednesday.

JOE. Wednesday?

JENNY. Wednesday.

JOE. Why?

JENNY. WHY!?

JOE. What?

JENNY. WHAT?!

JOE. Wow!

JENNY. Joe. The candles are dead.

JOE. What?

JENNY. And you murdered my rose.

JOE. I just wanted to say Happy Birthday.

JENNY. Thanks. (*To audience.*) The party was a lot of fun.

GROUP. (*Loud and boisterous.*) HA HA HA HA HA.

JENNY. I mingled. (*SHE stands in the center of the group.*) We talked about politics.

PARTY MEN. Can you believe those Republicans?

PARTY WOMEN. Can you believe those Democrats?

JENNY. (*To group.*) It's terrible.

ALL. Terrible is right.

JENNY. (*To audience.*) We talked about finance.

PARTY WOMEN. Can you believe what's happening to the stock market?

PARTY MEN. What about the yen?!

JENNY. (*To group.*) It's terrible.

ALL .Terrible is right.

JENNY. (*To audience*.) We talked about religion.

ALL. Do you believe in God?

JENNY. (*To audience*.) Who are they and why are they asking me this? We talked about nuclear weapons.

PARTY MEN. They're so bad.

PARTY WOMEN. Yeh, they're not good.

PARTY MEN. We shouldn't have them.

PARTY WOMEN. And what about the children?

PARTY MEN. What about the children?

ALL. Yes! What about the children?!

JENNY. (*Exploding to audience*.) Whose children?! I don't have any children. It takes two to make children—and Joe has deprived me of my natural born right to bear!!! (*Calming*.) Not that I wanted little Joe babies, but ... Suddenly I started feeling barren and sick—really sick and really barren. So I started drinking—and—I started feeling better. So relaxed—without a care. (*Heads back to Group*.) And then everybody started coupling off.

(The GROUP couples off.)

JENNY. The prime women were snatched up quickly and whisked away to little beds, leaving me alone with—

(All the MEN at the party begin swarming Jenny.)

JENNY. The Wolves of the One-Night-Stand. (*JENNY is tossed from one to the other*.)

WOLF 1. Isn't it terrible what's happening in politics. I have a waterbed. Would you like to go sailing?

WOLF 2. I've always admired your work. My roommate's out of town.

WOLF 3. I love you. I've always loved you and my body is aching to express that love to the only woman I love.

WOLF 1. Hey, whatta ya say you and me find a dark corner and—

JENNY. You're married!

WOLF 1. So's my wife.

JENNY. And then came King Wolf.

(The WOLVES scatter and wimper away.)

JOE. Hi, Jenny.

JENNY. Hi, Joe.

(JOE kisses her.)

JENNY. Joe—everybody's watching.

(CROWD stares.)

JOE. Nobody's watching.

(CROWD back to normal. JOE kisses her again.)

JOE. Do you need somebody to walk you home? *(Pulls Jenny closer.)* Well? Do you need somebody to walk you home?

JENNY. I only live a couple blocks away.

JOE. It's late. You're alone.

JENNY. I've walked home late and alone for the past two months.

JOE. Not this late.

JENNY. (*To audience.*) I could smell a one night stand.

JOE. Come on. (*Kiss.*)

JENNY. (*To audience.*) I could have been strong.

JOE. Let me walk you home.

JENNY. (*Pushing him violently.*) No, Joe, no.

JOE. Come on. (*Kiss.*)

JENNY. (*To audience.*) I could have been cool.

JOE. Let me walk you home.

JENNY. (*To Joe.*) What do you take me for?!

JOE. Come on. (*Kiss.*)

JENNY. (*To audience.*) I could have at least been cute.

JOE. Let me walk you home.

JENNY. (*Giggly.*) I don't know, Joe—are you sure you're just walking me home?

JOE. Come on. (*Kiss.*)

JENNY. (*To audience.*) But no-no-I. I felt a power. I could do it! One night with me. This was my chance to let him discover how much he loves me. (*Caressing him from behind, etc.*) I will speak his language and he will hear me. I will mesmerize him. I will break down his walls. I will free the incredible lover inside him. Our bodies will celebrate one another. And in the morning I will have someone to lean over and kiss me and someone to lean over and kiss. (*Ends with kiss.*)

JOE. Let me walk you home.

JENNY. (*Blankly.*) Sure, Joe, sure. If you really want to.

(*JOE starts off ahead of Jenny. SHE tries to keep up.*)

JOE. Come on, come on. You're lagging.

(The MAILMAN intercepts.)

MAILMAN. Hey, Jenny. Here's a copy of *Old Yeller*. I
think you'll—
JOE. *(Laughing.) Old Yeller?*

*(JENNY is embarrassed, takes book and leaves the
mailman alone. JOE and JENNY freeze on opposite
sides of the bed, facing one another.)*

MAILMAN. *(To audience.)* If you want it badly enough
you can get. I wanted Jenny. She was on my route. *(HE
picks up the daisy and exits.)*

(JENNY and JOE begin crawling into bed.)

JENNY. You're beautiful.
JOE. Yeah, yeah, yeah, you're beautiful too.
JENNY. Your eyes are so blue.
JOE. Yeah, yeah, you've got eyes too.

*(JOE is over her. Three swift motions: BANG BANG
BANG, and HE drops down asleep.)*

JENNY. *(From under his sleeping body.)* It was
beautiful!—because we said so—*(Sitting up.)* because what
else is there to say? And I was beautiful—because he said
so. He slept and continued making male sounds. I touched
his face and pretended I was in a poem. I felt right. I

watched him. (*Whispers.*) Joe, did you know that when I was seven years old I fell upside down from a swing onto a pile of bricks. It bled, Joe. It bled bad. (*HE murmurs.*) I knew he was dreaming of me—reliving the ecstasy. And then all at once—(*HE snores.*)—I knew he was just asleep. And then as I waited, I had the rare opportunity to watch myself be snuck out on.

(*JOE gets up, gathers his things and sneaks out.*)

JENNY. I closed my eyes, put my mind on rewind— (*JOE returns to the bed.*)—and ... *again* I watch myself be snuck out on. Only this time it hurt just a little bit more. STOP! SIT DOWN!

(*JOE sits stage right.*)

JENNY. I needed time to think. This isn't fair. A haver for half a night—I invested forty-five days in this guy. Why is he leaving? Why? (*JENNY runs to the chart #4 titled "Why Is He Leaving?"*) Okay, why is he leaving? (*SHE writes:*) A: Because—
JOE. I had a previous engagement.
JENNY. Why didn't you just leave a note?
JOE. Didn't have a pen.
JENNY. (*To Group now Jury.*) That's possible. I believe that.
JURY. (*Laughing.*) No. No. No. No. No. No No.
JENNY. (*Back to chart.*) Okay, B: Because—
JOE. I knew you wouldn't love me in the morning.
JENNY. Oh, but I would have.
JOE. No. No. You wouldn't have.

JENNY. Oh, yes, I would have. I was even going to make you pancakes.

JOE. If only I could believe that.

JENNY. (*To Jury.*) Oh, see, he's just a wounded little animal, and he needs me.

JURY. Noooo!

JENNY. Okay, C: Because—

JOE. I don't like you.

JENNY. You don't like me?

JOE. I don't like you.

(JENNY and JOE look to Jury.)

JURY. (*Enthusiasm building. Clapping.*) Good answer. Good answer! Good answer! Good Answer! GOOD ANSWER!

JENNY. (*Feeling a bit silly.*) Then why'd you come over?

JOE. A man has needs—and you let me.

JENNY. I let you because I like you.

JOE. Like me?

JENNY. Love you.

JOE. Love me?

JENNY. Worship you.

JOE. Worship me?!

JENNY. Like you a lot.

JOE. Why?

JENNY. (*Caught up in love.*) Why? Why?!—Because you're so—

JOE. Cold—

JENNY. Cold and—

JOE. —mysterious.

JENNY. Mysterious. And you make me feel so—
JOE. Stupid—
JENNY. Stupid and—
JOE. —ugly.
JENNY. —ugly. And you treat me like—
JOE. Trash—
JENNY. (*Elated.*)—trash the way I've always dreamed
of being treated.

(Stunned SILENCE. Jenny's bubble bursts.)

GROUP. So—why do you like him?
JENNY. My God—I have no idea.

(Female PROSECUTOR steps forward.)

PROSECUTOR. The prosecution rests, your honor.
JUDGE. Is counsel prepared for closing arguments?
PROSECUTOR. Yes, your honor.
JUDGE. And the defense?
DEFENSE ATTORNEY. Yes, your honor.
JUDGE. The defendant will please be seated.

*(JENNY looks to Joe waiting for him to sit. HE doesn't
budge.)*

JUDGE. I asked that the defendant please be seated.

*(Again JENNY looks to Joe questioningly. SHE indicates
him, HE indicates back to her.)*

JUDGE. Ms. Brown, will you please be seated!

JENNY. (*Stunned.*) Oh, you've got to be kidding?! (*JENNY sits.*)

JUDGE. Counsel may proceed.

DEFENSE ATTORNEY. (*Sympathetically pats Jenny on the shoulder, then with great bravado:*) Ladies and gentlemen of the jury, although it may be true that my client took part in a one night stand, my client—

JENNY. It was not a one night stand ... just a very short relationship.

GROUP. Yeh, right.

DEFENSE ATTORNEY. My client should not be on trial here. Oh no no no no no. We all know who the guilty party is. Oh yes yes yes yes we do. All you have to do is ask yourselves: Who ignored this woman and made her crawl?! (*Bravado gesture to Joe.*) This pig!

JENNY. Yeah, but—

DEFENSE ATTORNEY. (*Steam-rolling ahead.*) Who stood her up with no explanation?! (*Gesture.*) This Pig!

JENNY. Yeah, but—

DEFENSE ATTORNEY. Who took advantage of her weakened vulnerable state?! This PIG!

JENNY. Yeah, but—

DEFENSE ATTORNEY. And who snuck out when his fun was done?!!! (*Motions Jury to join in.*)

JURY. (*All caught up.*) THIS PIG!

DEFENSE ATTORNEY. That's right! That's what this pig did.

(*THEY hiss at Joe.*)

DEFENSE ATTORNEY. My client is innocent. My client was merely a victim.

JURY. (*Reacting to "victim."*) Ew.

DEFENSE ATTORNEY. (*Continues right along.*) That's right. A victim—

JURY. Ew!

DEFENSE ATTORNEY. (*A bit distracted and confused by reaction.*)—of this pig. So please, do the right thing: find her "Not Guilty." See her for what she is: An innocent ... Victim!

JURY. (*Shuddering.*) Eeeeew!

(*Defense Attorney steps back bewildered, not sure where he went wrong. Sounded good to him.*)

PROSECUTOR. (*Stepping forward.*) People, good fair people of the jury. The defense would like you to believe that in finding Ms. Brown guilty, you would be finding Joe innocent. This is not, however, the case. And the defense has greatly assisted me in establishing the fact that Joe is indeed a Pig.

JOE. Hey—for every man who is a pig, there's a woman out there who's glad he is.

PROSECUTOR. So if this pig sickens you as he so very sickens me, find Ms. Brown guilty, and let the only victim here be Joe, a victim of himself.

JUDGE. Has the jury reached a verdict?

(*Quick JURY murmur.*)

JURY FOREMAN. We have, your honor.

JUDGE. Will the defendant please face the jury?

JURY FOREMAN. We the Jury, find the defendant guilty of low self-esteem. (*GROUP gasps.*) Self-

deprecation, (*Gasps.*) and aiding and a ... bedding a pig.
(*Gasps.*)

    JUDGE. So say you all?

    JURY. Uh-huh.

    JUDGE. Bailiff, please tell Ms. Brown what she's won!

*(GAMESHOW HOSTESS steps forward and tosses
microphone to BAILIFF.)*

    BAILIFF. (*Placing winner's hat on Jenny's head.*)
Congratulations Jenny, you are our grand prize winner.
But, first let's take a look behind Door #3 to see what
you've passed up:

*(GAMESHOW HOSTESS gestures proudly toward
HYSTERICAL WOMAN who is clinging and grabbing
at boyfriend.)*

    HYSTERICAL WOMAN. (*Crying and sputtering.*) But
where were you? And where are you going?! Why can't I
go with you?! I'm sorry. I'm sorry. Was it something I
said? Something I did? Something I didn't do—didn't say?
What? What? What?!

    BAILIFF. "A FUTURE OF PIGWORSHIPPING!"

    GROUP. Aaaawwww!

    BAILIFF. And you also passed up Door #2:

*(GAMESHOW HOSTESS now gestures toward: WIFE
talking on the phone with her drunk HUSBAND beside
her.)*

WIFE. (*On phone.*) No, Mom, he really means it this time. He's quit drinking for good.

BAILIFF. "A LIFETIME OF DENIAL."

GROUP. Ooohhh!

BAILIFF. And now for the grand prize: It begins with a lifetime supply of self-help books—

(GAMESHOW HOSTESS presents bundle of books tied up in a red ribbon.)

BAILIFF. —which will certainly come in handy, because, yes, Ms. Jenny Brown, you —are—going—to—THERAPY!

(APPLAUSE and SHOUTS of joy from GROUP. JENNY is ecstatic.)

BAILIFF. Where you will marvel at the depths of your problems, visit the ego, the id—as well as the seven wonders of your personality.

(GAMESHOW HOSTESS, out of props, gestures on herself for the seven wonders. "Oooh's" and "Aaah's" from the GROUP.)

JUDGE. This court hereby sentences you to two years of therapy with no chance of parole. (*Hammers gavel.*) Case dismissed.

JENNY. (*Fully charged.*) I served my sentence! Paid my dues! Attended my sessions and learned that—(*Goes to easel.*) I had been caught in a vicious cycle—(*Chart #5.*) I had starved my ego—(*Chart #6.*) I had been holding on to a painful past. (*Chart #7. Runs to books—rummaging through them—showing the titles as she goes.*) I read the books and learned that I was a WOMAN WHO LOVED TOO MUCH in search of my INNER CHILD. I was a SMART WOMAN making FOOLISH CHOICES, falling for MEN WHO CAN'T LOVE but loving them anyway. And WHEN I'D SAY NO I'D FEEL GUILTY preventing me from becoming one of the WOMEN MEN LOVE but instead one of the WOMEN MEN LEAVE. But, I came to know MY MOTHER and know MYSELF. I learned that I'M OKAY and YOU'RE OKAY. I came UP FROM DEPRESSION. I studied the LOVE CODES and made an active decision that with or without a man, I would suffer NO MORE LONELY NIGHTS. For years, voices had been clamoring in my head:

(*GROUP all talks at once as JENNY conducts them.*)

GROUP. You're stupid, you're ugly, etc.
JENNY. But after two years of therapy—

(*Signals GROUP to stop.
SILENCE.*)

JENNY. Do you hear that? I don't either. Isn't it wonderful? Now I can come home and appreciate the silence. And I don't have to worry about blasting my music and missing something, 'cause I know they're out there.

(*A look of concern comes over JENNY—SHE opens the door. THREE MEN scurry to her door just in time. Big smiles. JENNY waves.*)

JENNY. Just checking. (*Closes door.*) And now when I close my eyes, I can imagine this place as it's going to be.

MAILMAN. (*On bed, reading from book.*) "Old Yeller was his name. The name had kind of a double meaning..."

JENNY. (*Opens eyes, surprised.*) Mailman? (*To audience, throwing hat skyward à la Mary Tyler Moore:*) I'll be right there.

(*LIGHTS down as SHE runs into his arms.*)

THE END

PROPERTY LIST

Seven chairs
Bed w/pillow
Waste basket
Bench
Piano (Optional. To accompany Lounge Singer.)
Four roses
Two books (*Cujo*)
Book (*Old Yeller*)
Easel (for charts)
Hat
Mail bag
8 letters w/envelopes
Pen
Magic Markers
Newspaper
Mutant-sized daisy
Beer bottles
Two glasses
Long-stemmed rose
Bundle of self-help books.
Microphone

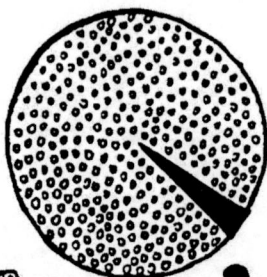

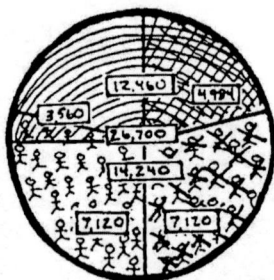

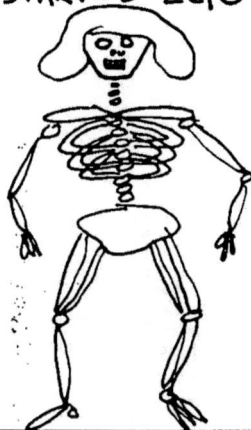

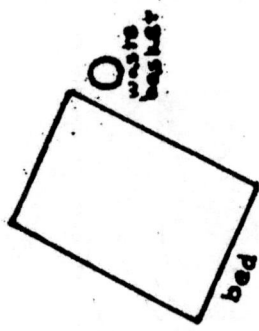

bed

white blanket

easel

tape deck

chairs

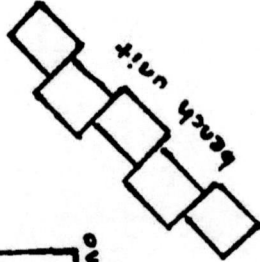

bench unit

piano